Angela Merkel
Chancellor of Germany

by Kate Moening

BLASTOFF! READERS
2

IA · MINNEAPOLIS, MN

Note to Librarians, Teachers, and Parents:

Blastoff! Readers are carefully developed by literacy experts and combine standards-based content with developmentally appropriate text.

Level 1 provides the most support through repetition of high-frequency words, light text, predictable sentence patterns, and strong visual support.

Level 2 offers early readers a bit more challenge through varied simple sentences, increased text load, and less repetition of high-frequency words.

Level 3 advances early-fluent readers toward fluency through increased text and concept load, less reliance on visuals, longer sentences, and more literary language.

Level 4 builds reading stamina by providing more text per page, increased use of punctuation, greater variation in sentence patterns, and increasingly challenging vocabulary.

Level 5 encourages children to move from "learning to read" to "reading to learn" by providing even more text, varied writing styles, and less familiar topics.

Whichever book is right for your reader, Blastoff! Readers are the perfect books to build confidence and encourage a love of reading that will last a lifetime!

This edition first published in 2020 by Bellwether Media, Inc.

No part of this publication may be reproduced in whole or in part without written permission of the publisher. For information regarding permission, write to Bellwether Media, Inc., Attention: Permissions Department, 6012 Blue Circle Drive, Minnetonka, MN 55343.

Library of Congress Cataloging-in-Publication Data

Names: Moening, Kate, author.
Title: Angela Merkel : Chancellor of Germany / by Kate Moening.
Description: Minneapolis, MN : Bellwether Media, Inc., [2020] | Series: Blastoff! Readers: Women Leading the Way |
    Includes bibliographical references and index. | Audience: Grades K-3. | Audience: Ages 5-8.
Identifiers: LCCN 2018053537 (print) | LCCN 2018054899 (ebook) | ISBN 9781618916709 (ebook) | ISBN
    9781644870983 (hardcover : alk. paper) | ISBN 9781618917218 (pbk. : alk. paper)
Subjects: LCSH: Merkel, Angela, 1954–Juvenile literature. | Prime ministers–Germany–Biography–Juvenile literature. |
    Women prime ministers–Germany–Biography–Juvenile literature. | Heads of state–Germany–Biography–Juvenile
    literature. | Women heads of state–Germany–Biography–Juvenile literature.
Classification: LCC DD290.33.M47 (ebook) | LCC DD290.33.M47 M64 2020 (print) DDC 943.088/3092 [B] –dc23
LC record available at https://lccn.loc.gov/2018053537

Editor: Al Albertson   Designer: Andrea Schneider

Printed in the United States of America, North Mankato, MN.

Table of Contents

Who Is Angela Merkel?

Angela Merkel is the first woman to become **chancellor** of Germany.

She is one of the most important leaders in the world!

Angela's workplace

"WHEN IT COMES TO HUMAN DIGNITY, WE CANNOT MAKE COMPROMISES." (2011)

Angela grew up in **East Germany** in the 1960s. People there could not leave or share certain ideas.

Templin, Germany
Angela's hometown

N
W E
S

Angela learned that freedom
is important!

Getting Her Start

Angela was a smart, quiet student. She was driven to learn.

Angela studied **physics** after high school. She became a **scientist**.

Angela Merkel Profile

Birthday: July 17, 1954

Hometown: Templin, Germany

Industry: politics

Education:
- physics degree (University of Leipzig)
- chemistry degree (German Academy of Sciences)

Influences and Heroes:
- Horst Kasner (father)
- Marie Curie (scientist)
- Catherine the Great (empress of Russia)

In 1989, East Germany became free! East and West Germany became one country in 1990.

Angela became a **politician** to help the new country grow.

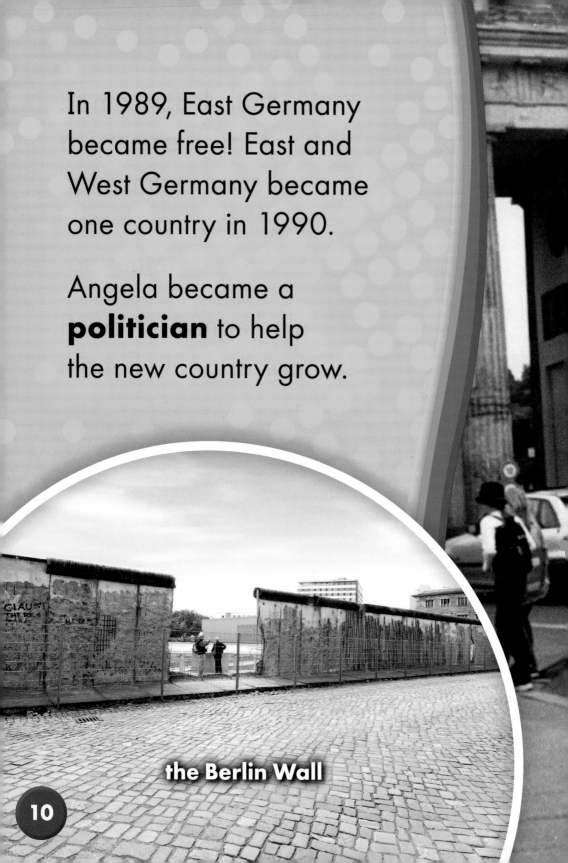

the Berlin Wall

"I'VE NEVER UNDERESTIMATED MYSELF. THERE'S NOTHING WRONG WITH BEING AMBITIOUS." (2010)

Changing the World

Many politicians were loud and bold. But Angela was quiet and **patient**.

Leaders trusted Angela.
They **appointed** her
to important jobs.

**Angela meeting with
the leader of Spain**

In 1999, Germans found out Chancellor Kohl had lied. He took money he should not have.

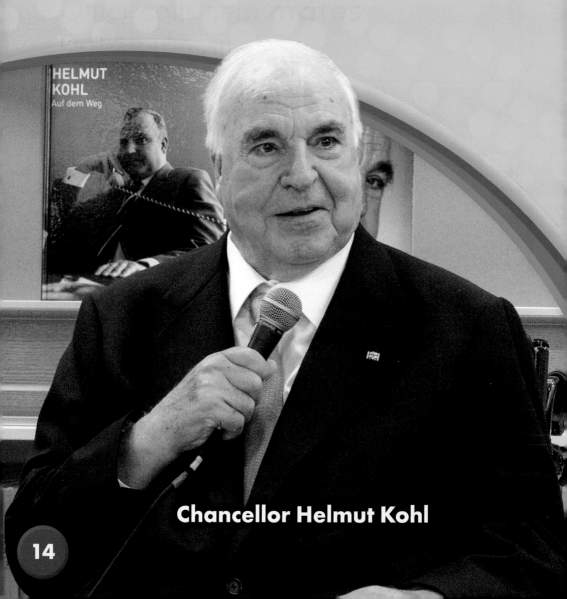

Chancellor Helmut Kohl

Angela spoke out
against him! She won
the Germans' trust.

In 2005, Angela was **elected** chancellor. She was a smart leader.

When other countries **struggled** with money, Angela kept Germany strong.

Angela being sworn in as chancellor

Angela with French President Emmanuel Macron

Angela's Future

Angela won her fourth **term** in 2017.

Angela Merkel Timeline

1989   Angela begins working with the group Democratic Awakening after East Germany is freed

1990   Angela wins her first seat in the German government

1999   Angela writes an article against Chancellor Helmut Kohl for stealing money

2005   Angela is elected chancellor of Germany

2018   *Forbes* magazine names Angela the "World's Most Powerful Woman"

nd,

Only two other chancellors have led Germany as long as she has!

Angela plans to step down in 2021. She will make room for a new leader.

Angela wants **democracy** for all. She knows freedom is important!

"FREEDOM DOES NOT MEAN BEING FREE OF SOMETHING, BUT TO BE FREE TO DO SOMETHING." (2015)

Glossary

appointed—chose for a job or duty

chancellor—the head of the German government; the chancellor in Germany is like the president in the United States.

democracy—a government where people have equal rights and choose their leaders by voting

East Germany—a country that existed between 1949 and 1990 that is now part of present-day Germany; Germany became one country again after the Berlin Wall that separated East and West Berlin came down.

elected—chosen by voting

patient—calm and careful when waiting for a long time

physics—a science that deals with matter and energy and the way they act on one another

politician—someone who is active in government

scientist—a person who is trained in science and whose job involves doing research or solving scientific problems

struggled—worked at something that was hard

term—the period of time that an elected politician holds office

To Learn More

AT THE LIBRARY

Cole, Tom Clohosy. *Wall*. Somerville, Mass.: Templar Books, 2014.

Dean, Jessica. *Germany: All Around the World*. Minneapolis, Minn.: Pogo Books, 2019.

Leaf, Christina. *Michelle Obama: Health Advocate*. Minneapolis, Minn.: Bellwether Media, 2019.

ON THE WEB

FACTSURFER

Factsurfer.com gives you a safe, fun way to find more information.

1. Go to www.factsurfer.com.

2. Enter "Angela Merkel" into the search box and click Q.

3. Select your book cover to see a list of related web sites.

Osage City Public Library
515 Main Street
Osage City, Kansas 66523
www.osagecitylibrary.org

Index

The images in this book are reproduced through the courtesy of: SULUPRESS.DE/ Marc Vorwerk/ Alamy, front cover (Angela); canadastock, front cover (Germany), p. 3; patrice6000, front cover, pp. 3, 23 (flag); Rolf G Wackenberg, p. 4 (inset); Alexandros Michailidis, pp. 4-5; Sueddeutsche Zeitung Photo/ Alamy, p. 6; Ulrich Baumgarten/ Getty, pp. 8; 360b, pp. 9, 20-21; gary718, p. 10 (inset); ullstein bild/ Getty, pp. 10-11; DanielW, pp. 12-13 (top); Pool Moncloa/Fernando Calvo, p. 13 (bottom); Markus Wissmann, p. 14 (bottom); Ronny Hartmann/ Getty, pp. 14-15 (top); JOHN MACDOUGALL/ Getty, p. 16 (inset); WENN US/ Alamy, pp. 16-17; Jan von Uxkull-Gyllenband, pp. 18-19; imageBROKER/ Alamy, p. 20 (inset).